How to Sparkle at

WRITING
STORIES AND POEMS

Irene Yates

Brilliant Publications

We hope you and your class enjoy using this book. Other books in the series include:

Maths titles

Science titles

English titles

Festive title

Published by Brilliant Publications
Unit 10, Sparrow Hall Farm, Edlesborough, Dunstable, Bedfordshire LU6 2ES
Sales and stock enquiries   Tel: 01202 712910
                             Fax: 0845 1309300
                             Email: brilliant@bebc.co.uk
                             Website: www.brilliantpublications.co.uk
General enquiries: Tel: 01525 222292

The name Brilliant Publications and its logo are registered trade marks.

Written by Irene Yates
Illustrated by Kate Ford
Cover illustration by Sue Woollatt

Printed in the UK

© Irene Yates 1997
ISBN 978 1 897675 18 2

First published in 1997
Reprinted 1998, 1999, 2007
10 9 8 7 6 5 4

Contents

Introduction

This book will help early and beginning writers to master some of the skills of composition and writing conventions.

All of the activities stimulate creative writing, in the form of story or poetry. They are designed to give children lots of ideas and to help them to plan and develop those ideas. On many of the sheets lines have not been drawn in. This is a deliberate ploy on the writer's part to allow the sheet to be used by children working at different levels. For example, a five year old child may only be able to fit one or two lines of writing in between the choruses of one of the poems, whereas a seven year old may be able to fit in four or five. You should use your knowledge of the children's ability to encourage the child to produce a response appropriate to his or her level.

Each of the sheets incorporates a 'Colour the star if …' activity. These are extension tasks to help develop the children's thinking on the main task and to give the task a further functional purpose. Many of these tasks will, hopefully, lead you and the children into further ideas for extension work.

Some of the star activities encourage the children to think of different audiences for their writing. You may like to extend this idea by discussing with the children whether the writing changes when it is written for different purposes and different readers. For instance, will the task remain the same when the child writes for an adult as for when the child writes for a younger child? This idea of audience awareness is one that can be cultivated from a very stage, even though it may not be assimilated until much later. To begin with, it may make very little difference to the actual product, however the concept of writing for a specific audience will grow with time and constant reinforcement, so that by the time the writer reaches the later levels of writing attainment, he or she will have a good perception of what difference the intended reader can make to the writing, which will make all the difference to the child's later understanding of the interaction of language and literature.

As all the sheets are photocopiable, the children may use them first to make their drafts on and then do follow-up drafts on scrap paper. You may wish to provide them with a clean copy of the sheet on which they can do their final copy. The children should not be limited by the amount of space on the page. Encourage them to continue their story or poem on the back of the page or on a blank sheet of paper.

How to use this book

The activities in this book are designed to fit in with any language scheme that you follow.

They can be used with individual children or with small groups, as the need arises. The text on each page has been kept as short as possible so that early readers will feel confident to tackle the activities without too much teacher input. On the other hand, some children may require you to read through the page carefully with them before they embark on the activity.

The order in which the pages are arranged is not particularly the order in which they should be used. A flexible approach and a knowledge of the sheets will provide the teacher with a bank of ideas that will help the children to extend their writing skills.

How children write is often determined by the quality of the discussion they take part in before the writing begins. Beginning writers often need to verbalise all their ideas before committing them to paper. This helps them to clarify and sequence them. Some children may not suggest any ideas at all and in such cases ideas that other children offer during discussion should be shared and developed.

Many of the sheets can be used as models, which you will be able to develop further. The poetry sheets, in particular, are good for this because they give the idea of a 'form' which may then be applied to different topics.

Before the children tackle the tasks independently, it is sometimes a good idea to go through the activity together, on a board of some kind, so that the children then have a model on which they might base their own work.

In order to be well motivated to write, children need to have good reasons for writing. You can provide some reasons by 'publishing' the writing in:

- individual writing folders. Each child collects their pieces of written work in a folder. The children should be given the opportunity to arrange the work in the order which they want it read and be encouraged to make up a contents list. You could use the title and contents pages provided on pages 8 and 9 of this book.

- class books or anthologies. Collect all the children's work on one topic, together. Bind the work together and make a cover with sugar paper. Brainstorm a good title with the children. Get the children to illustrate the book and to write their names on the contents page.

- individual books. The children can collect several pieces of their own work together, bind them into a book and make a cover. Again, they will need to make a contents page, give the book a title and perhaps have an 'about the author' page.

Most writing is done with the expectation that someone will read what has been written – it is good for the children to be able to share their work, and to invite other people to read it. This makes them feel that it has some value, and builds up the willingness and confidence to keep writing.

Links to the National Curriculum

This book fits in with the National Curriculum programme of study for Key Stage 1 Writing by offering practice in:

1   Range

a   Pupils should be helped to understand the value of writing as a means of remembering, communicating, organising and developing ideas and information, and as a source of enjoyment. Pupils should be taught to write independently on subjects that are of interest and importance to them.

b   Pupils should be given opportunities to write in response to a variety of stimuli, including stories, poems, classroom activities and personal experience. Pupils should be taught to identify the purpose for which they write and to write for a range of readers, *eg their teachers, their family, their peers, themselves.*

2   Key Skills

b   Pupils should have opportunities to plan and review their writing, assembling and developing their ideas on paper and on screen. Teachers should, on occasion, help pupils to compose at greater length by writing for them, demonstrating the ways that ideas may be recorded in print. To encourage confidence and independence, pupils should be given opportunities to collaborate, to read their work aloud and to discuss the quality of what is written. Pupils should be helped to make choices about vocabulary and to organise imaginative and factual writing in different ways, *eg a cumulative pattern in a poem.*

Extension ideas

The following activities will help to extend the tasks given in this book, in order to broaden children's experience and add to their writing ability.

- Build up individual word books so that the children don't have to keep asking for spellings. Encourage the children to enter words in their books that they use frequently and to look them up before asking. Wall boards also offer the children a lot of encouragement. Group words by topic content, or by grammatical functions – ie verbs, adjectives, nouns. Alternatively group words that have the same letter strings – ie *fight, sight, light*.

- Have read-aloud sessions in which some children have the opportunity to read out their writing to the rest of the class. If someone is too shy to read then ask if you may read their writing for them.

- Use the children's written work for class assemblies and for presentations to small audiences of other children or parents.

- Make a point of displaying some new written work regularly, say every week. Have a notice board that shows 'Writing of the week'. This may be chosen by you, or by agreement with the children as work is read aloud. Try to make sure that every child eventually gets a chance.

- Encourage parents to help their children with writing by being a good audience and resisting the urge to correct every error. Explain to them how the children have to 'crack the code' of written language and how praise encourages them to do so more than 'marking' every mistake does. Help them to see that focusing on one area of learning at a time builds up the children's skills.

- Build up a 'writing centre' in your classroom which contains lots of writing tools, different kinds of paper and card, and lots of different safe stationery items such as a hole punch, stickers, stamps and inkpads.

- Have a 'story wall' which is a public display area of the children's writing. Cover a board with attractive paper and give all the children the opportunity to display some form of writing. Let them decide what they want to share and get them to contribute items for the story wall on a voluntary basis. Encourage positive feelings about the work, regardless of what stage of writing the child is at.

My Creative Writing Folder

In this folder
You will see
Stories and poems
Written by ME!

I am _____

Class _____

Year _____

Contents page

These are the stories and poems in my
Creative Writing Folder.

Page

_____

_____

_____

_____

_____

_____

_____

_____

What can I write about?

This is a list of topics that I could write stories or poems about. Every time I think of a new topic I write it down. This way I never run out of ideas.

1 <u>New bike</u>   16 _____

2 <u>Ducks, ducks, ducks</u>   17 _____

3 <u>A rainbow</u>   18 _____

4 <u>Family celebration</u>   19 _____

5 _____   20 _____

6 _____   21 _____

7 _____   22 _____

8 _____   23 _____

9 _____   24 _____

10 _____   25 _____

11 _____   26 _____

12 _____   27 _____

13 _____   28 _____

14 _____   29 _____

15 _____   30 _____

Colour the star if you have so many ideas that you need another page.

Planning a story

My topic is:

At the beginning I will tell about:

In the middle:

At the end:

My characters are:

Colour the star if you can write a story from your plan for a friend.

I like writing

Best of all I like writing ...

When I write a story, I think about ...

When I write a poem, I think about ...

The best story I have written is called ...

It is best because ...

Colour the star if you can think of three people you could write stories and poems for.

My best story

My best story is called ...

It is good because ...

My favourite part is ...

I could make it better by ...

Colour the star if you can make your best story even better.

At the park

What can you see? What is happening? Tell the story for your teacher to write.

_____

_____

Copy the story here.

_____

_____

Colour the star if you can read your story to the teacher.

Skating penguins

What can you see? What is happening? Tell the story for your
teacher to write.

_____

_____

Copy the story here.

_____

_____

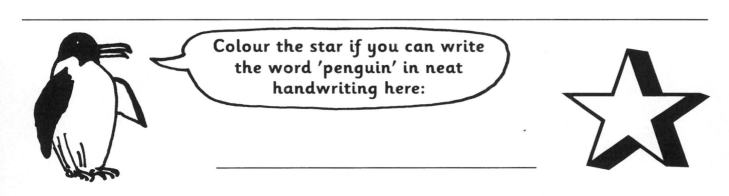

Colour the star if you can write
the word 'penguin' in neat
handwriting here:

_____

On the planet Ogg

What can you see? What is happening? Tell the story for your teacher to write.

_____

_____

Copy the story here.

_____

_____

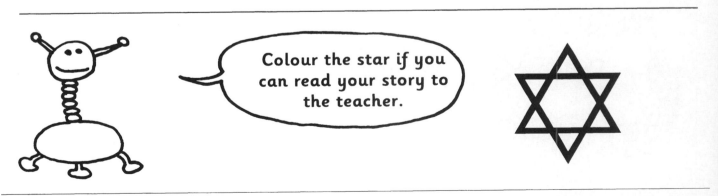

Colour the star if you can read your story to the teacher.

Best friends

Who are they?

Why are they so happy?

Where have they been?

What have they done?

Why are they best friends?

Write the story here:

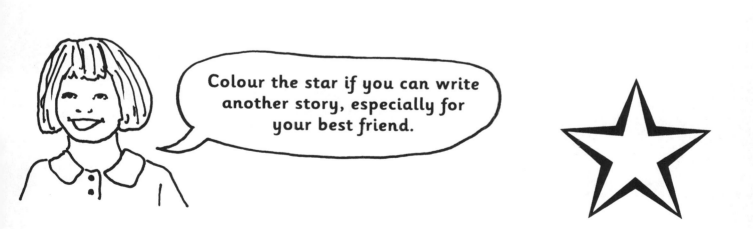

Colour the star if you can write another story, especially for your best friend.

Thank you

Think about:

Who are they?

Who is saying 'thank you'? Why?

Where are they?

How did they get together?

What adventure have the two had together?

Write the story here:

I'm sorry

Who are they?

Who is sorry? Why?

What has happened?

What happens next?

Write the story here:

Colour the star if you can draw a clown on the back of the page.

If I was

If you were not you, who would you like to be?

Somebody you know? A super hero? A special kind of person?

I would be:

Think of what would happen.

Write your story here:

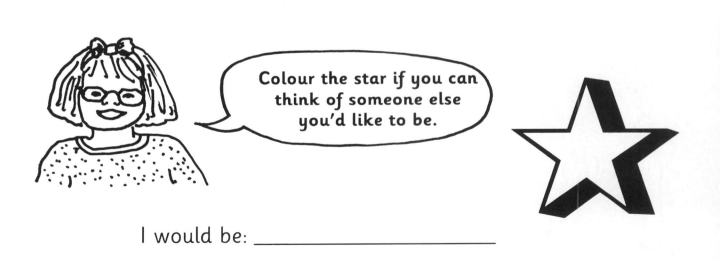

Colour the star if you can think of someone else you'd like to be.

I would be: _____

Space adventure

In the box is a very special spacesuit just for you.

Open the box carefully. Put on the spacesuit.

Climb into your spaceship and ... off you go!

Write your story here:

Colour the star if you can write another space story, especially for someone in your family.

Ben's adventure

This is Ben.

He's got nothing to do and no one to play with. Don't let him get bored! Make up a friend for him and send them off on an adventure!

Write your story here:

Colour the star if you can read the story to a friend.

Help!

Imagine one day you go to school and just as you go in, everything shrinks. Except you! Suddenly everything is tiny and you're a great big giant! What do you do?

Write what happens here:

Colour the star if you can write another story about a giant, especially for someone who goes to your school.

The Dreaded Dragon

The Dreaded Dragon has come to town. The people are frightened and run away. They hide in their houses. But along comes someone to save them. Who?

Write the story here:

How to Sparkle at Writing Stories and Poems
24

The crystal palace

This magic palace shimmers and shines in the sunlight. You see it has a 'For Sale' sign. You go inside to have a look.

Write a story about what you find here:

Colour the star if you can read your story to a friend.

Joey's first jump

Once upon a time there was a little kangaroo who couldn't jump. He was very unhappy.

All the other kangaroos could jump high in the air. But no matter how hard Joey tried, his feet just stayed on the ground.

Then, one day ...

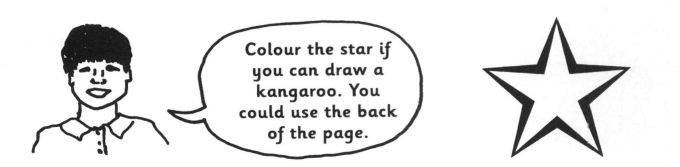

Colour the star if you can draw a kangaroo. You could use the back of the page.

Pirate Pete

This is Pirate Pete. He is sailing on a big ship across the seas. Pirate Pete is looking for an island with a cave. He wants to hide some treasure in the cave.

What happens?

Write your story here:

Colour the star if you can draw a treasure chest full of jewels. You could use the back of the page.

Time to hatch

Here are some eggs.

They might belong to:

Oh, oh – the eggs are beginning to hatch!

Whose eggs are they? What happens next?

Colour the star if you can write another egg story for someone younger than you!

A wonderful surprise

This a Tammy. In a minute she is going to get a really wonderful surprise.

What's the surprise?

What will happen?

Write your story here:

Colour the star if you can write a story about the best surprise you ever had. You could use the back of the page.

Magical powers

Suppose you had the power of magic. You could do anything you wanted to do. You could make all your wishes come true.

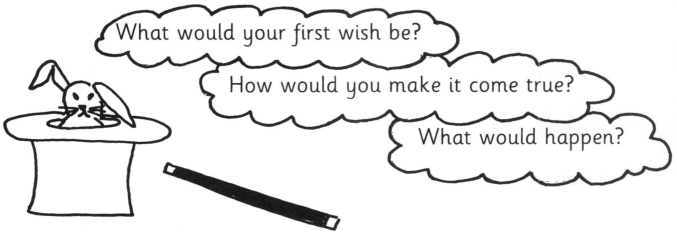

What would your first wish be?

How would you make it come true?

What would happen?

Write the story here:

Colour the star if you can make up a magic spell and write it here.

Helpful Harriet

This is the mouse family.

This is Harriet. She is a really helpful mouse.

Sometimes Harriet helps too much. Give the family names and then tell the story of how Harriet's helping caused a problem!

Colour the star if you can draw Helpful Harriet. You could use the back of the page.

Holiday

Write the story here:

Colour the star if you can share your story with a friend.

You could use some of these words:

beach	build	caravan	castle
fun	holiday	ice cream	paddle
sand	sea	seaside	spade
summer	sunshine	swim	waves

The snowman

Write the story here:

Colour the star if you can tell someone how to build a snowman.

You could use some of these words:

bare	big	boots	build
deep	eyes	garden	hat
little	melt	nose	scarf
snow	snowman	thick	white

Escape!

Write the story here:

You could use some of these words:

bird	cat	escape	flies
food	grass	hide	hungry
looking	pouring	pounce	pulls
rain	ready	watching	worm

Colour the star if you can read the story to someone else.

Follow that bike!

Write the story here:

Colour the star if you can write another story about a dog.

You could use some of these words:

ball	bike	dog	follow
friend	going	home	park
play	ride	sit	stay
stop	street	sunshine	together

Cats

You can write a cat poem.

Cats

Cats have kittens who play all day,

Cats

Cats have whiskers and long, long tails,

Cats

Cat are cuddly and like to purr,

Cats

Colour the star if you can read your poem to a friend.

Dazzling dream

Write a poem about an exciting dream you might have had.

Fast asleep,

I had a dream that ...

Fast asleep,

I had a dream that ...

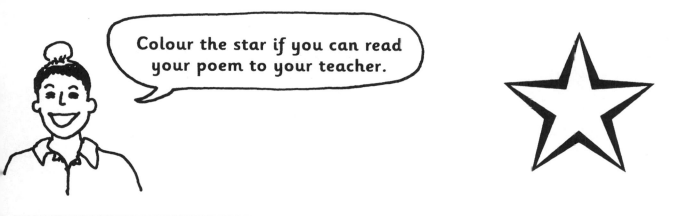

Colour the star if you can read your poem to your teacher.

Dawdling ducks

When ducklings grow big enough, their mum leads them to the pond for their first swim.

Write a poem about it.

Come on, quacks the Mother Duck

Waddle, waddle, waddle.

Come on, quacks the Mother Duck

Splish, splosh, splash.

Colour the star if you can write a poem about another creature. First decide who to write it for.

Sunshine

S unny days are

U sually very

N ice.

Write an acrostic poem.

S
U
N
N
Y

Colour the star if you can write another **SUN** poem. You could use the back of the page.

Rainy days

R ain comes down in cats

A nd dogs,

I nside it's dry, but outside it's

N ot.

Write an acrostic poem.

R
A
I
N
Y

Colour the star if you can draw a picture of it raining cats and dogs. You could use the back of the page.

Snow time

 S nowflakes

N ever settle

O n

W et boots.

Write an acrostic poem.

Colour the star if you can make a snowflake using a piece of paper and some scissors.

Thunder and lightning

S tormy days bring

T hunder and lightning all

O ver the sky –

R oaring and

M agnificent.

Write an acrostic poem.

T
H
U
N
D
E
R

Colour the star if you can write an acrostic poem for **LIGHTNING.** You could use the back of the page.

Precious things

Everybody has precious things. What is your most treasured thing?
Why is it precious? Where did it come from? How do you keep it
safe?

Write a poem about your treasure.

My treasure is ...

I always keep it safe.

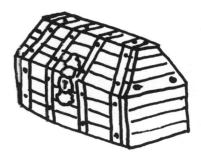

My treasure is ...

I always keep it safe.

Colour the star if
you can write six
words to describe
your precious thing.

Alphabet poem

Write a supermarket poem:

At the supermarket we see

A

B

C

D

E

F

G

H

At the supermarket we buy

I

J

K

L

M

N

O

P

At the supermarket I see apples, bananas, cakes...

At the supermarket we see

Q

R

S

T

U

V

W

X

At the supermarket we buy

Y

Z

Colour the star if you can write an alphabet poem for the zoo.

Shape poems

Read these shape poems.

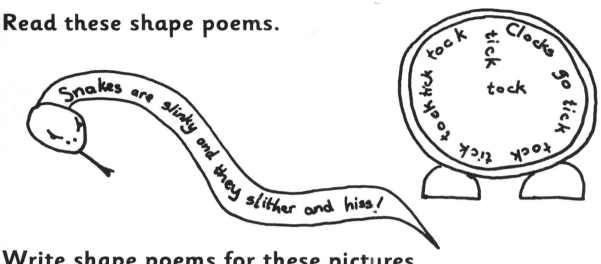

Write shape poems for these pictures.

Colour the star if you can read your shape poems to a friend.

Feelings

Sometimes we feel good, sometimes bad.
Sometimes happy, sometimes sad.

Write a poem about those times.

Sometimes I feel happy

happy, happy, happy.

Sometimes I feel sad

sad, sad, sad.

Sometimes I feel really good

good, good, good.

And sometimes I feel bad

bad, bad, bad.

Colour the star if you can write about other feelings you have.

Christmas magic

Write a Christmas story or poem.

Colour the star if you can find the word 'turkey' on this page.

You could use some of these words.

baubles	born	carol	December
decorate	decorations	happy	Jesus
manger	merry	presents·	reindeer
Santa	singing	sleigh	stable
star	tree	turkey	year

Happy holidays

Write a holiday poem or story.

You could use some of these words.			
aeroplane	beach	bucket	boat
caravan	ferry	going	happy
luggage	kite	seaside	shell
spade	sunshine	suitcase	swim
tent	travel	waves	wind

Colour the star if you can write a postcard from the holiday.

Dear

To:

love from,

Lightning Source UK Ltd.
Milton Keynes UK
UKOC01f1525131113

220973UK00002B/9/A